RAINBOW COLORS

Library of Congress Number: 84-26250

3 4 5 6 7 8 9 10 11 12 13   96 95 94 93 92 91 90 89

Printed and bound in the United States of America

Library of Congress Cataloging in Publication Data

Kirkpatrick, Rena K.
 Rainbow colors.

 (Look at science)
 Includes index.
 Summary: Simple text and illustrations introduce
the colors of the rainbow.
 1. Rainbow—Juvenile literature. [1. Rainbow]
I. Title. II. Series.
QC976.R2K57   1985   551.5′67   84-26250
 ISBN 0-8172-2356-8 (lib. bdg.)
 ISBN 0-8172-2381-9 (softcover)

RAINBOW COLORS

By Rena K. Kirkpatrick
Science Consultant

Illustrated by Anna Barnard

Raintree Childrens Books
Milwaukee

What is a rainbow?

    A rainbow is an arch of color in the sky. You may see a rainbow after it rains. Sunlight shining through raindrops makes a rainbow.

Where do you look to see a rainbow?
    If you put your back to the sun, you
can see a rainbow. Sometimes there
are two rainbows. The colors are
brighter in the lower rainbow.

Where else can you see rainbows?
Water sprinklers throw drops of
water into the air. When the sun
shines on the drops, you will see a
rainbow. The drops split the sunlight
into colors.

Have you ever blown soap bubbles?
   You can see rainbows on the bubbles.
   Bubbles also split light into colors.

Can other things make rainbows?
You can see rainbows in oil spots on wet roads. Sometimes you can see a rainbow in a piece of glass or on the edge of a mirror.

What can a fish tank do to sunlight?
When the sun shines through the
corner of a fish tank and the water,
the light is split into colors. If you
stand in the right place, you will see a
rainbow.

How can you make a rainbow?
Put a dish of water in a sunny place.
Then hold a mirror in the water so
that the sun hits it. Move the mirror
slowly until you see a rainbow on the
ceiling.

What happens when the water moves?
Stir the water with your finger. The
colors disappear from the ceiling.
When the water stops moving, the
colors will come back.

How many colors are in a rainbow?
Usually, you see four or five colors in
a rainbow. But if you look carefully,
you can see seven. They are red,
orange, yellow, green, blue, indigo,
and violet.

pointed stick

stiff card

What happens when colors spin together?
Make some tops. Then put different
colors on them. When you spin the
tops, you will see new colors.

How many green things can you see?
Green is a rainbow color. Many
things in nature are green. Some
fruits and vegetables are green.
Sometimes they change to another
color after they get ripe.

How many red things can you see?
Red is also a rainbow color. There
are many different kinds of red. We
call each kind a shade.

How many colors can you find in nature?
There are many more colors in
nature than the seven rainbow colors.
Flowers have many colors. They add
beauty to yards and homes.

What do nature colors do in the fall?
Many colors of nature change in the fall. Leaves change from green to red or yellow or brown. You can look for ripe berries and fruit in fall.

Have you every watched a dragonfly?
A dragonfly has very thin, delicate
wings. They shine in the sunlight.
You can see rainbow colors on a
dragonfly's wings.

tiger
moth

common
blue
butterfly

peacock
butterfly

ladybugs

wasp

Do insects have many different colors?
Insects add lots of color to nature.
They have colorful patterns. Look for
insects. See how many different
colors you can find.

woodpecker

parakeet

How are birds colored?
Male birds usually have bright and
colorful feathers. Female birds
usually have dull-colored feathers.

How do things get colored?
You can use paint to make chairs or tables colorful. Dyes make cloth things colorful.

Which box is harder to see?
    The white box is easy to see. It is
    very different from the green leaves.
    If you paint the box green, it is much
    harder to see.

What animals do you see on this page?
Animals' colors and stripes look like
ones in nature. Animals are safer
when they are hard to see.

Which colors blend?
   Some colors go well together. We say
   they blend. Brown and yellow blend.
   Black and gray blend. Name other
   colors that blend.

What are contrasting colors?
Red and green are very different
colors. We say they are contrasting
colors. Contrasting colors may go
well together, too. Red and black
contrast. What other colors contrast?

What does colored light do to things?
The light from these street lights is
yellow. The yellow light makes a
white house look yellow. Yellow light
makes a green car look black.

shoe box

flashlight

tissue paper

How can you make things change color?
Put colored things on a stage. Then
find colored tissue paper. Cover a
light with the paper, and shine it on
the stage. How do the colors on the
stage change?

red
plastic

colored
glass

How does colored glass change things?
Some things seem to change color
when you look through colored glass
or plastic. Not all colors change. A
red object still looks red through a
red glass.

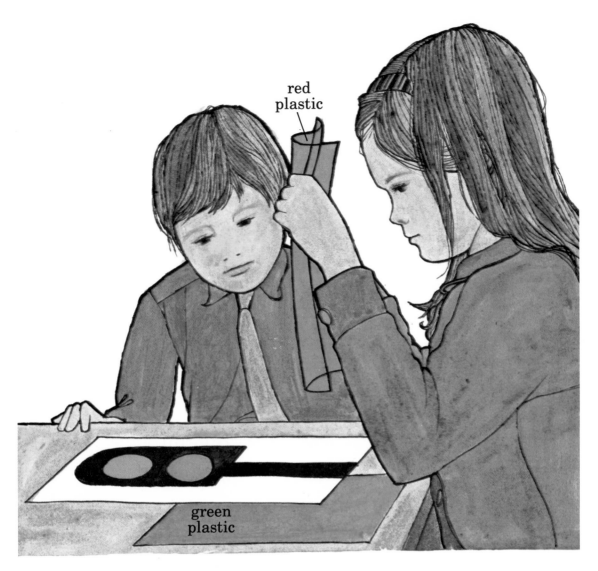

red
plastic

green
plastic

Can a light change from red to black?
Look at a traffic light through red
plastic. The red looks red, but the
green looks black. Through green
plastic, the red looks black, and the
green looks green.

Look at Rainbow Colors Again

You can see a rainbow after it rains.

A rainbow is made when sunlight shines through raindrops.

You can see rainbows in many places.

Water drops and other things split sunlight into colors to make rainbows.

The rainbow colors are red, orange, yellow, green, blue, indigo, and violet.

There are many colors in nature.

Paints and dyes can make things colorful.

Insects and other animals have many colors.

Some animals are hard to see because of their colors.

Some colors blend.

Some colors contrast.

Colored light makes some colors look different.

Look at These Questions About Rainbow Colors

1. When can you see a rainbow?

2. What makes a rainbow?

3. What can water drops do to sunlight?

4. How many colors are in a rainbow?

5. What happens when some fruits get ripe?

6. What makes you see rainbows on a dragonfly's wings?

7. What is paint used for?

8. Why are some animals hard to see?

9. What does colored light do to things?

10. What happens to a green light when you look through red plastic?

Words in RAINBOW COLORS

sprinkler
page 6

bubble
page 7

oil
spot
page 8

mirror
page 8

dish
page 10

stir
page 11

berries
page 17

pattern
page 19

stripes
page 23

flashlight
page 27